midnight f[...]
HEATHER SORENSON

3   Travel Light

11   Let Me Walk You Home

19   Now I Lay Me Down to Sleep

25   Nightlights

36   My Midnight Faith

44   Things We Remember

47   Raise Your Hands

54   I Have Loved the Stars Too Fondly

62   Be Still My Soul

67   Day Is Dying in the West

To access OBBLIGATO PDFs visit:
www.halleonard.com/mylibrary

Enter Code
1813-1103-6471-9969

ISBN 978-1-5400-4157-9

EXCLUSIVELY DISTRIBUTED BY

Visit Hal Leonard Online at
www.halleonard.com

Visit Shawnee Press Online at
www.shawneepress.com

Contact us:
Hal Leonard
7777 West Bluemound Road
Milwaukee, WI 53213
Email: info@halleonard.com

In Europe, contact:
Hal Leonard Europe Limited
42 Wigmore Street
Marylebone, London, W1U 2RN
Email: info@halleonardeurope.com

In Australia, contact:
Hal Leonard Australia Pty. Ltd.
4 Lentara Court
Cheltenham, Victoria, 3192 Australia
Email: info@halleonard.com.au

FOREWORD

I'm rarely given inspiration for a song that I've not first had to live. I live each song twice: once in real life, and once again as I write the music. Writing a project titled *Midnight Faith* was no different. For the last few years, I've been fascinated with the metaphor of nighttime, specifically in how it pertains to our lives. I learned to understand darkness. There are people whose nighttime is temporary and brief; there are people who live in the night for years. But what about the people who never leave the darkness, the ones who have been called to live in the night? Maybe they are the stars who shine for others; and in their own night, they become a light for those passing through the darkness. The first line of the title song speaks to the inspiration for this project: "Faith looks different in the dark."

– Heather Sorenson

ABOUT THE COLLECTION

Midnight Faith is a true concept project. Stylistically diverse, this collection has a running thread of a nighttime theme which seams these original songs together into one cohesive work. Using her unique signature approach to songwriting, Heather combines different genres together to create a blend of sound that is characteristic of her music as she ventures into folk, Christian, jazz, original classical, and her own singer-songwriter style.

ABOUT THE ARTIST

Heather Sorenson is a Dallas songwriter and composer, whose works are performed in churches, universities and concerts worldwide. She is contracted by Hal Leonard, the largest print music publisher in the world, and has hundreds of compositions in print through various publishing houses. Initially recognized for her skill as a pianist, she is now widely known for her choral, piano and orchestral works. Heather has appeared multiple times at Carnegie Hall, Lincoln Center and Constitution Hall.

in memory of Homer and Myrtle Stanbery

TRAVEL LIGHT

vocal solo, opt. vocal trio, with opt. fiddle*

Words and Music by
HEATHER SORENSON (ASCAP)

Leave all your cares, and leave all your woes. Lay down your bur - dens, lay down your load. Fol - low your path un - til it is done. Turn from your wor - ry. Turn to the Son. Then you will find __ that

* Part for Fiddle available as a digital download.
www.halleonard.com/mylibrary

you can trav - el light.

Cast - ing all your care up - on the Lord of Light,__ 'fess-

-ing up your sin so you can sleep at night,__ of - f'ring up some help to the

peo - ple on your way;__ that's how you trav - el light.

(opt. trio)

Rec - og - nize the good when the day is bright.__ Lean__ in - to the rough, and you will be al - right.__ Let - ting go the things that were nev - er yours to claim;_____ that's how you trav - el light.

Watch for the curves, but cruise when you can.

Reach for the stars, but don't o - ver plan. Share what you know, and

learn from the best. Do what you can. Let God do the rest.

Then you will find __ that you can trav - el light.

Leave all your cares, and leave all your woes. Lay down your bur - dens,

lay down your load. Fol - low your path un - til it is done.

Turn from your wor - ry. Turn to the Son. Then you will find that

you can trav - el light. Cast-

-ing all your care up-on the Lord of Light,__ 'fess - ing up your sin so you can

sleep at night,__ of - f'ring up some help to the peo-ple on your way;__

that's how you trav-el light. Rec -

- og-nize the good when the day is bright.__ Lean__ in - to the rough, and you will

for my dear friends Tranessa, Amy, and Heather
who have walked me through life

LET ME WALK YOU HOME

vocal solo, with opt. violin and cello*

Words and Music by
HEATHER SORENSON (ASCAP)

Maybe we've got years to go, or maybe time is short. The journey is important though, and we all need some support. In

* Parts for Violin and Cello available as a digital download.
www.halleonard.com/mylibrary

Where two___ or three___ are gath - ered, we make___ a might - y choir!___ I will take the low___ notes, and you___ can take___ the high-er. It's not___ a race___ to heav - en, but if___

you get there first, _____ I'll

hand you off__ to Je - sus, and I'll sing an-oth - er verse,_ I'll

sing an-oth - er verse.____ So let me walk you

home. Let me walk you home to Je - sus. He's run-

- ning out __ to meet __ us, and His smile lights up the way. __ Let me walk you

home. We can make this road a sanc - tu - ar - y, a ha -

- ven for __ the wea - ry, and be - fore we know, __ the time __

__ has flown. We blink __ our eyes, __ the years __

May - be we've got years to go, or may - be time is short. The

jour - ney is im - por - tant though.

Let me walk you home. Is there

some - thing I can car - ry?

dedicated to my friend, Lori Adams

NOW I LAY ME DOWN TO SLEEP

with Angels Watchin' Over Me

vocal solo

Words by
HEATHER SORENSON
based on a traditional children's prayer

Music by
HEATHER SORENSON (ASCAP)

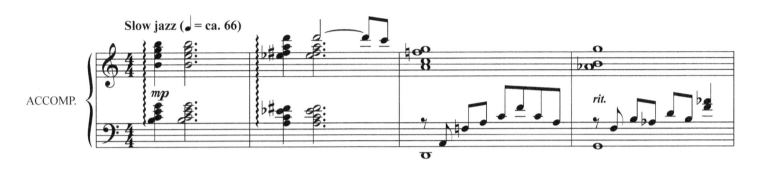

1. Now I lay me down to sleep. I pray the Lord__ my
2. Mat-thew, Mark, and Luke, and John, please bless the bed__ I

soul to keep.__ If I should die be-fore I wake,
sleep up - on.__ There's one to watch, and one to pray.

* Tune: ALL NIGHT, ALL DAY, traditional spiritual

an - gels,___ an-gels, they are watch-in' o - ver me.___

An - gels,___ an - gels, they are watch - in' o - ver me.___

rit.

rit.

dedicated to my "Atlanta Pastor," the Rev. James Ward

NIGHTLIGHTS

piano and cello*

Music by
HEATHER SORENSON (ASCAP)

* Part for Cello available as a digital download.
www.halleonard.com/mylibrary

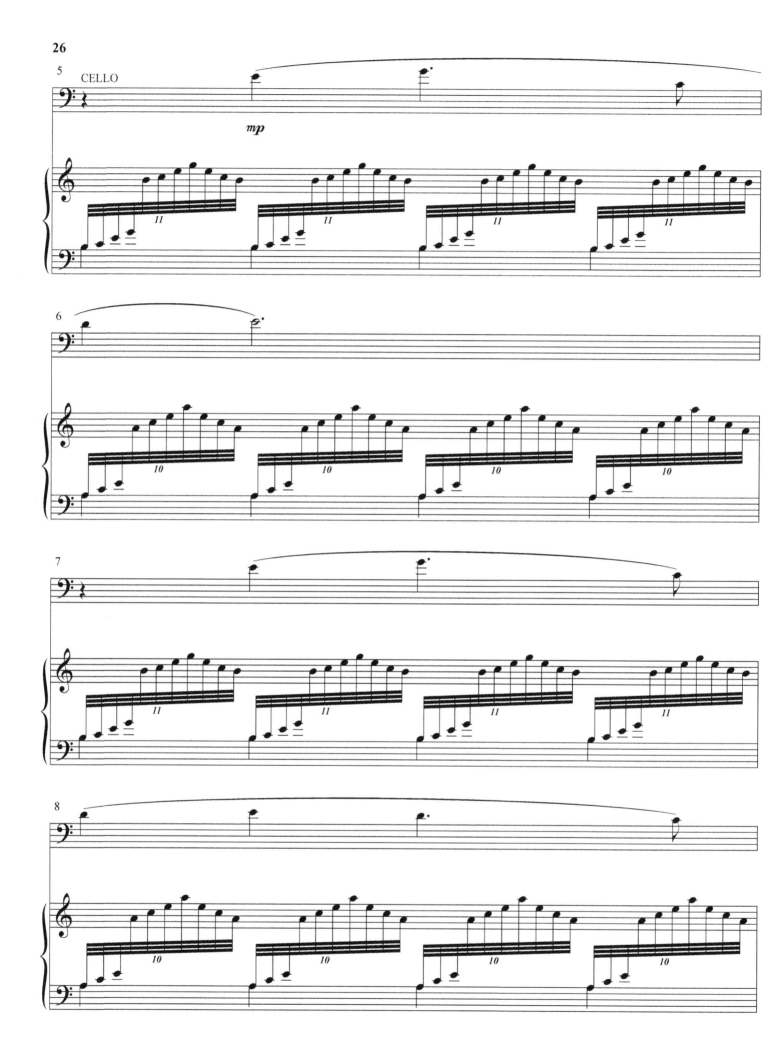

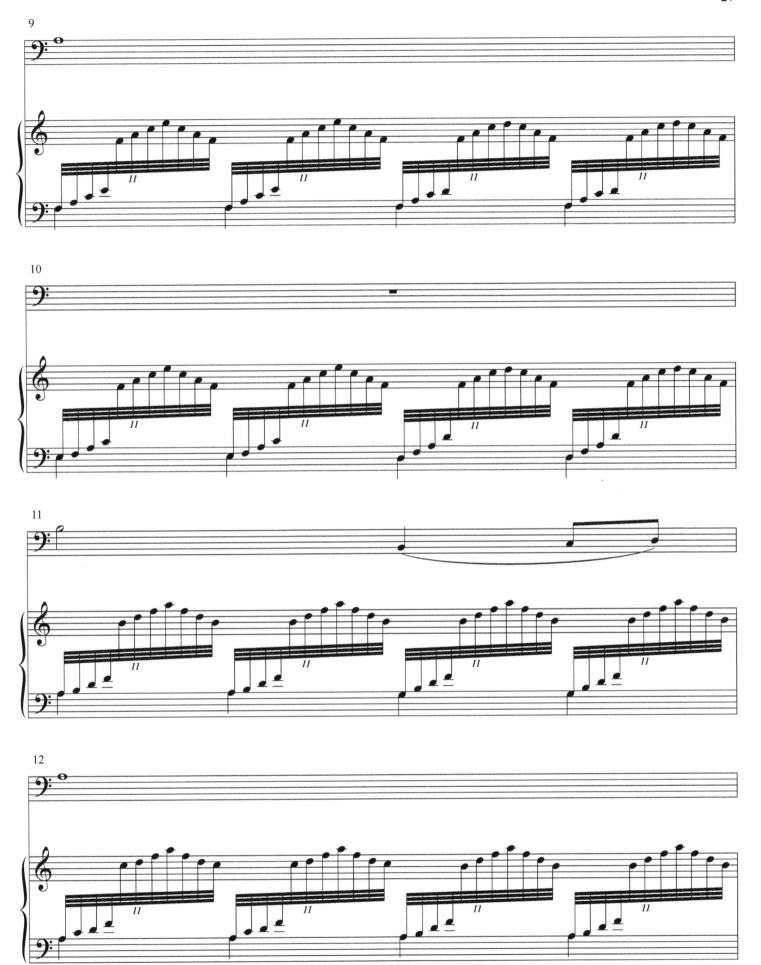

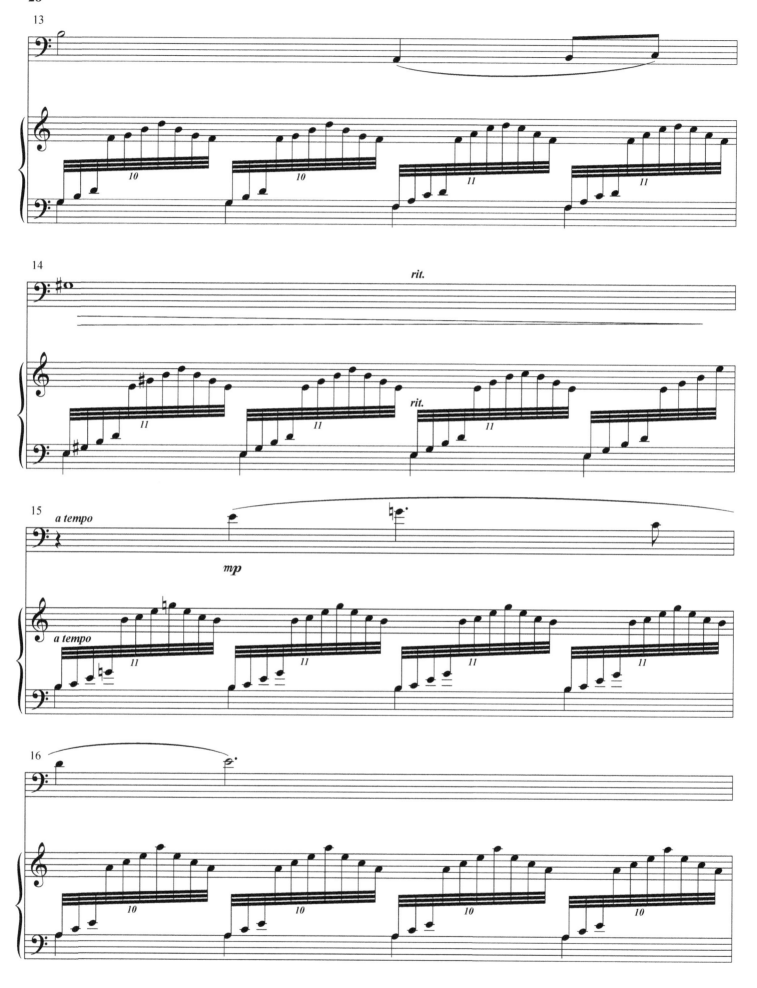

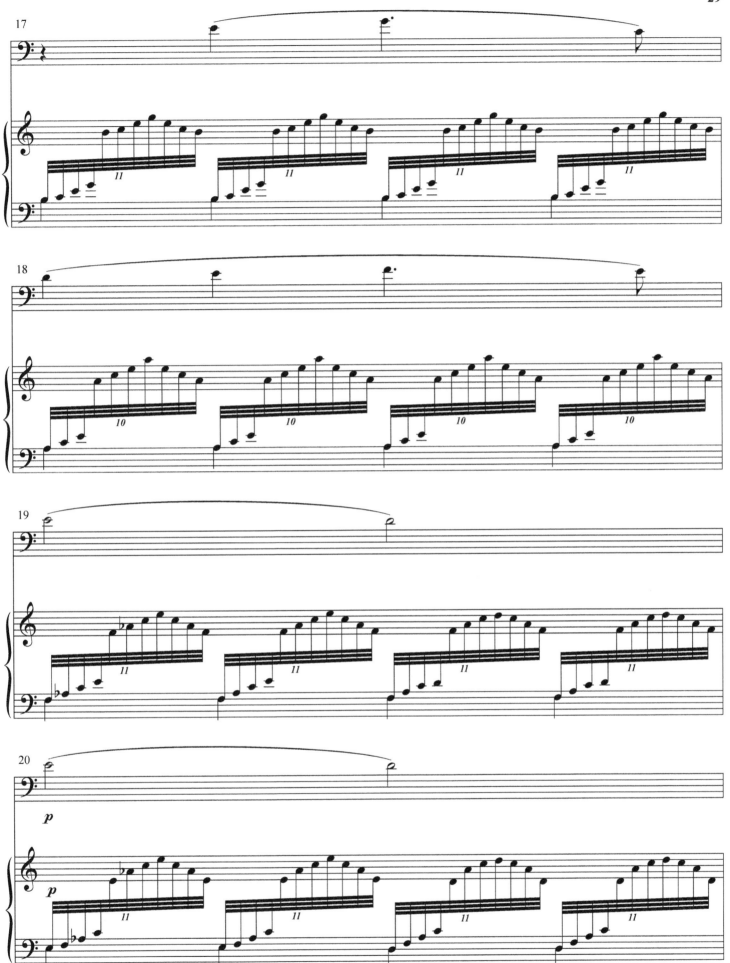

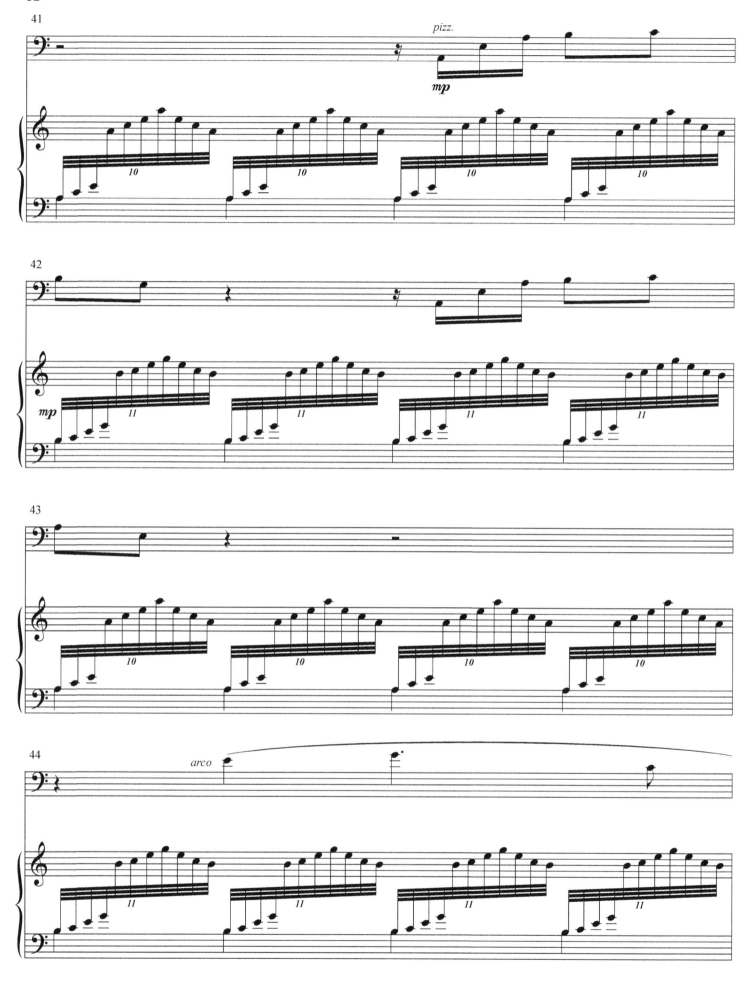

34

MY MIDNIGHT FAITH

vocal solo, opt. vocal trio

Words and Music by
HEATHER SORENSON (ASCAP)

Faith looks dif-f'rent in the dark.

Grace looks dif-f'rent now that I'm the one who's cov-ered in marks.

Faith kneels long-er when it's been through the war,

Structured

Faith claims vic - t'ry in___ the dark.

Grace claims heal - ing for the

life that sin___ has bro - ken a - part.___ Faith grows deep - er when it's

put to the test;___ some dreams left un - met,___ still no re - grets.___ I

said I'd keep___ my eyes___ on You,___ oh, Fa - ther of ___ Lights.___ I

thought that it___ was dark___ out, but then, then You sent the night,

then You sent the night. This is my mid-night___

___ faith. ___ This is me ask - ing for grace, ___ grace, ___

in memory of Carl and Wilma Weaver

THINGS WE REMEMBER

piano solo

Music by
HEATHER SORENSON (ASCAP)

RAISE YOUR HANDS

vocal solo

Words and Music by
HEATHER SORENSON (ASCAP)

Raise your_____ hands to the One who gives_ us ev - 'ry-thing,_ yet He

shines in emp - ti - ness._____

More steady

Raise your_____ hands when you're

of - f'ring up_ the sac - ri - fice_ that you want to claim_ as yours._

Raise your _____ hands, reach- ing up___ to heav - en _____ when your

heart's bowed to the floor. ___ Raise your _____ hands,

trust - ing in___ the grace___ of God___ that has car - ried you___ be - fore. _____

___ I will lift___ my hands___ to You, ___ and bless Your name___ for - ev -

heart is full of wor - ship, and your songs are filled with praise.

Raise your hands when the bat - tle ends in vic - t'ry, and God's

glo - ry is a - blaze. Raise your hands. Let the

earth shout "Hal - le - lu - jah!" and the peo - ple shout "A - men!"

And the

hands that have __ been emp - tied, _____ God will fill them once a - gain. __

I will lift___ my___ hands to You.___

I will lift___ my___ hands to You.___

And the hands that have___ been emp - tied,___ God will

Slowly

fill them once a - gain.___ Raise your___ hands.

dedicated to Richard Hampton

I HAVE LOVED THE STARS TOO FONDLY

vocal solo, with opt. violin and cello*

Words by
HEATHER SORENSON (ASCAP)
Quoting from the poem "The Old Astronomer"
by SARAH WILLIAMS (1837-1868)

Music by
HEATHER SORENSON

I've felt the wind that breaks the ship blow gen - tly on my

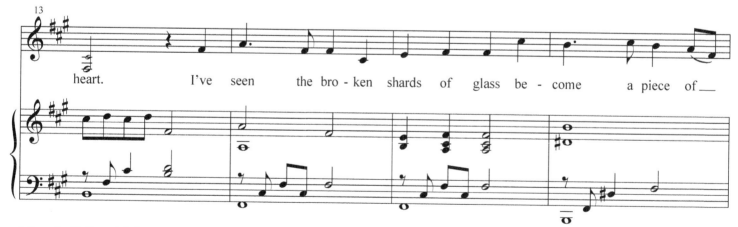

heart. I've seen the bro - ken shards of glass be - come a piece of __

* Parts for Violin and Cello available as a digital download.
www.halleonard.com/mylibrary

I've heard the an-gel's greet-ing be the mourn-er's song of death.__ I've known the air that brings new life to take a-way my__ breath. I've watched the shad-ows turn to black and o-ver-take the light, but I've loved the stars too fond-ly to be

fear - ful of the night._____ Sun - light

fades. Light I love has__ dimmed. Bright - ness, once a -

blaze, now flick - er - ing a - way. Mid - night

comes rid - ing on the__ wind._____ Though my

soul may set in dark-ness, it will rise in per - fect light. I have

loved the stars too fond - ly to be fear - ful of the night,

the night. If dark - ness comes at

e - ven - tide, or if it dims the morn, my path is bright, ce -

Though my soul may set in dark-ness, it will rise in per-fect

light. I have loved the stars too fond-ly to be fear-ful of the

night,_____ the night. I have

Slower, rubato (♩ = ca. 100)

loved the stars too fond-ly to be fear-ful of the night.

BE STILL MY SOUL

piano solo

Tune: **FINLANDIA**
by JEAN SIBELIUS (1865-1957)
Arranged by
HEATHER SORENSON (ASCAP)

DAY IS DYING IN THE WEST

vocal solo with opt. cello*

Words by
HEATHER SORENSON (ASCAP)
and MARY LATHBURY (1841-1913), *alt.*

Music by
HEATHER SORENSON

* Part for Cello available as a digital download.
www.halleonard.com/mylibrary

sky.   While the deep - 'ning shad-ows fall,   heart of love   en-fold - ing

all,   through the glo - ry and the grace   of the stars   that veil Thy

face,   our hearts as-cend.   Our hearts as-cend._____

Our hearts as-cend._____   We will

praise___ You, al - le - lu - ia, God of ev - 'ry star - ry night. All the

earth___ will bow be - fore___ You. You are heav - en's great - est Light.___

When for - ev - er from our sight, past the

stars, the day, the night, Lord of an - gels, on our eyes, let e - ter - nal morn-ing

rise, and shad-ows end, and shad-ows end.

Our hearts as-cend.

Day is dy - ing in the west. Heav - en touch - es earth with rest.

pp

* Tune: CHAUTAUQUA, William Fiske Sherwin, 1826-1888